Troubadour

The Best of Rhyme
at
the year, 2001

Published by

Towers and Rushing, Ltd
San Antonio, Texas

Troubadour – 2001

Editor/Publisher
Dr. Ron Ribble

Consulting Editor
Henry George Fischer

Troubadour is a journal dedicated to excellence and appeal in poetry. The journal follows the spirit of tradition.

Troubadour and its publishers, Towers and Rushing, Limited, do not assume responsibility for the views of its contributors nor for lost or damaged manuscripts. A report will be issued if a stamped, self-addressed envelope is included with submissions. Copies of all submissions ought to be retained. Poems must be original and unpublished—unless otherwise or specifically invited.

Address all correspondence to

Troubadour
Towers and Rushing, Ltd.
P.O. Box 691745
San Antonio, Texas 78269-1745

Table of Contents

Troubadour's PUSHCART Nominees For 2001
[Poems appeared in Troubadour – 2000]

David Stephenson for his poem, "Moths"
X. J. Kennedy for his poem, "Stickup"
J. Weintraub for his poem, "Looking Back"
Jill Williams for her poem, "The Many Sides of Silence"
David Hill for his poem, "The Blind Girl"
Henry George Fischer ..., "The Truth of Troubadours"

Publishers Commentary

There is a great deal to explore in this year's *Troubadour*. To be sure there is excellent poetry— some of it extraordinary. That's what *Troubadour* is about: good, well-crafted, accessible verse that has an impact. It isn't necessarily the case that a given reader will like it all but it's safe to say there is something here for everyone.

We are a passionate group of poets and publishers but we are not prejudiced. Every kind of poetry that is well written and meaningful should be celebrated. We feature the traditional, the formal...the rhyming verse because of its under-representation in most of the well-known literary journals. As James Ragan makes clear in his interview, the modernists and post-modernists have taken poetry largely away from the people and ensconced it in the halls of ivy and other such sophisticated arenas where it has been purified and elevated to an elite status—often devoid of anything remotely resembling its oral tradition.

Mind you we all have prejudices and those prejudices attest to the nature of our individual needs. I have personally heard and read certain poets disparage rhyme as the A-B-Cs of poetry, as learning the scales, as distracting, as jingly and primitive. And to be perfectly truthful there is an element of truth to all they claim, because what they complain about is the very essence of rhyme and its traditional popularity with the masses— folks who needn't be able to read to memorize and enjoy an artform that strikes a primitive human harmonic inside all of us.

To reject or ignore the primitive evolutionary vestiges that still steer human passion, mood and behavior is to be in denial of what we are—animals with great cognitive power and creativity. We have the potential to overcome all obstacles to our survival as a species or to destroy ourselves with little effort. It is our primitive nature—the seeds of which are buried deep within us— that fuels the most delightful and most dreadful parts of ourselves.

Rhyme, because it is rhythmic, is brother to music. Music that strikes a chord with us is easily learned and recalled in part because the music's rhythm or beat—it's timing—prompts anticipation. Poetry that strikes a beat does the very same thing. Brain researchers have noted that music sets up biochemical and electro-physiological changes deep in the most primitive brain regions that are gateways to one of the early phylogenetic aspects of human behavior, survival-related emotions such as joy, grief, anger, fear, etc. Some scientists suggest that the reason music moves us so much is that it mimics our species primitive communications calls…and, perhaps, strikes some harmonic frequency in us that leads us to anticipate what is to come.

Captives

No matter how long the earth has spun—
how different we've all become,
there's something that binds us heart and soul
to the primal beat of the drum.

Despite the marvels of our time,
the pull of the past prevails
over the progeny of our minds
which yield to those undulant trails
where all our species began its trek
on the simmering Garden floor

to a throbbing, hypnotic rhythm
that would drive us forevermore.

And, so, to this day when the impulse awakes
something buried inside of us hums,
and we are impassioned to do what we <u>must</u>
by those damnable, bestial drums.

But rhyme is not magic and rhythm can be tedious.
Therefore we should never believe a poem cannot break
stride and still be a wonderful poem. Mindless or strident
adherence to predictability takes that importance element
of surprise—of catching the reader off guard—away
from the poet. Thus you see verse in this year's book
which has strident rhythm and rhyme which apparently
has no rhythm—no prosody. You will also read verse
that is partially strident and partially aprosodic.
Furthermore you will find excellently written verse that
is as color rich and word rich as free verse, dispelling the
excuse that rhyme is somehow artistically limiting. It all
belongs; it's all rhyme.

In the end what's important about any piece of poetic
work is the particular impact it has on us cognitively and
affectively. And that, except for those particularly
notable great pieces of artwork, is largely a matter of
individual taste and those primitive little gremlins
lurking in the shadows of our souls.

An Interview of James Ragan

James Ragan is head of the Graduate Professional Writing Program at the University of Southern California. He is also widely recognized and acclaimed as a poet and writer, an interpreter and translator, a man for all seasons. He is a warm, likable and genuine person.

Ragan by choice has kept himself apart from those poetic and academic cliques whose forte is criticism and whose members extol and promote each other's work as true art. While his choice of remaining separate from such groups might disadvantage him in some ways, it has resulted in his being widely called on as a truly impartial judge of others' genuine poetic and written merit.

I have absolutely no doubt in my mind that James Ragan's work and judgment are driven by a philosophy that it is the poem not the style which achieves greatness and furthermore that the very best poetry deals with issues of substance in such a way as to be understood and relished by a wide variety of people.

Troubadour: Do you do your own translations from English to Czech and Czech to English?

Ragan: I've done it in the past with Slovak, which is really my native tongue. Most of my brothers and sisters were born in Czechoslovakia. I grew up in Pittsburgh. We spoke Slovak at home until my parents died a couple of years ago. I really began to speak English in the first and second grades and gradually learned to master English. It was common for me in my early writing days to translate some of my poems into Slovak and even read my poems in Slovak when appropriate for the audience.

Troubadour: Since you do translate, let me ask whether you think anything is lost in the process of translation?

Ragan: I think there is! I'll give you an example. When I translated and edited – with Albert Todd – the Yevteschenko collected poems, I found that the translators—all of them very good translators—who originally introduced his work to English-speaking folks had changed the form of his poems from quatrains or tercets to, say, one long stanza without line breaks. Then I realized that in his original Russian the images were much more striking, real, and fresh than the translations and in fact were often reduced to cliché in English. Of course, they were making him accessible to American audiences but you could easily see what was lost in translation. My job when I translate is to bring the translation as close to the original meaning in the work's native language even though a perfect translation is often not possible. I try to preserve the music—if there is music—the rhyme and the stanzaic structure.

From my own standpoint, if someone is translating my work, I don't mind if the translators sometimes miss. I am honored that someone thinks my work important enough to translate.

Troubadour: I think that my only reservation about the translation of poetry from other languages is when figurative or symbolic language is involved. The question I have is whether it is always possible to make a translation as powerful and meaningful as the original poem?

Ragan: Well I have noticed that when a translation of a poet's work such of that of Yevteschenko is done with the poet and a language scholar, side-by-side, collaborating in the process of translation that those poems usually come across powerfully and beautifully.

Troubadour: A change of pace—is there a kind of contemporary elitist notion that there are only certain kinds of poetry that are truly worthy of being called art?

Ragan: There is a lot of room for all kinds of poetry. I stand firm on that statement. I have so many students come into the classroom who want to write form and I say, "Go for it!" I have others who want to write free verse or prose poetry and my reaction is the same. There was a time, particularly between the 1920s and the 1950s, when there was an elitist movement, the New Criticism, that took poetry away from the populace and took it primarily into the classroom. Some people still follow that track.

In my endeavors I want to bring poetry back to the populace. I don't agree with any elitist notions about poetry…that good poetry is only of this kind or that kind. Poetry needs all of the different voices and all of the different avenues especially in a world that has become so media-oriented and cliché-ruled. We need poetry in all of its colors and kind to represent the highest level of communication.

Troubadour: I have a colleague who after she had read our first issue of Troubadour told me she had enjoyed certain elements of the journal but just couldn't get into the rhyme because she blocked the instant she spotted the end rhyme. My response to her [as a psychologist] was that her reaction was characteristic of a prejudice. I don't specialize in rhyme because it is the only acceptable poetry to me but simply because I don't believe there are enough quality journals that will print rhyme and there are so many folks who write rhyme and other formal poetry so well.

Ragan: Then you agree with me

Troubadour: Absolutely and without qualification

Ragan: This discussion reminds me of when I was in Moscow in 1985 along with Bob Dylan, Robert Bly, and other poets from around the world performing for Gorbachev and an audience of 10,000. I had a chance to walk through Boris Pasternak's house—then blocked to public access for political reasons—and I found myself in awe of his place, its Spartan simplicity and beauty, and was moved to write a poem about it. I said to myself, "My God I've just got to write a poem about this place." I envisioned an epic but the poem wouldn't allow itself to be more than a sonnet. Everytime I'd tried to extend the piece it came back to the sonnet. The poem took its own shape, ...its own form. It wouldn't allow itself to be otherwise. It occurs to me that you chase the poem until it catches you. Poetry—good poetry—takes its own shape and determines its own direction.

The Poem took its own shape, its own form. It wouldn't allow itself to be otherwise. Good poetry takes its own shape and determines it own direction.

Standing At Pasternak's Table
James Ragan

Birch bark, soundings in the linden wood,
ferns ornate as creweled cloth or filigree,
prints of birdscape in pastures and old sod—
These, like May light, he could not spare as easily
as I might, but memorized the Urals
in floats of geraniums unloamed from pots,
vowels of sunlight along the sill.
What the world had named, was neither poem nor art,
as if to walk in cadence were voiceless, doggerel
laced like shoes to slow his feet.
Words should grow inquisitive, becoming avowals,
as in birth or naming the unnamed, how brief
their passage of identity, yet precious
their fidelity to all natures voice

Peredelkino, 1985

4

Troubadour: How about one arcane question? What is the state of poetry today?

Ragan: I know people like Bob Pinsky and others are saying that poetry is alive and well but my fear is that we can be led astray to believe it's truly so. I really believe that those who are attending poetry readings and supporting poetry are other poets or students of poetry.

Troubadour...exactly

Ragan: So many of them have been attending graduate writing programs such as the one I direct at USC, that we are turning out a wonderful reading audience as well as writing audience. When I was in graduate school there were only about 18-20 writing programs across the country. Now there are about 288 such writing programs which means we are building an audience. But coming through the 60s and 70s as both of us have we really did see the populace. Perhaps, because of such things as the Vietnam War, civil rights, and ecology, we were more issue-oriented. You could command an audience of a thousand at that time but you really don't see that much of an audience now unless it's a major author doing the reading.   .

My feeling at the moment is there are so many distractions away from the arts that we are seeing some welcome efforts to bring back the audience poetry once had. In that sense I'm glad to see that the venues have multiplied, that the conglomerates like Borders and Barnes & Noble have instituted readings along with the college classrooms or the corner coffee shops. So we are building an audience but in a much more segmented way. It used to be that there were causes and issues and poets led those causes and issues. Thus while poetry is making a comeback I don't think we ought to be fooled into believing that there is anywhere near the involvement there once was.

Troubadour: When I offered a similar question to Bob Hass – but perhaps put too much emphasis on the <u>reading</u> of poetry –

he rejected the notion that poetry enjoyed a lesser audience today than years ago. I thought about the matter afterwards, talked with others, including my Latina wife and found that poetry was often a traditional oral way of passing on history and culture in the absence of the ability to read.

Ragan: Exactly. Poetry has its roots in the oral tradition. It began with the odes and antipodes of old Greek drama. The troubadours took that tradition further by going into the villages, entertaining, singing and speaking in verse. From those times on poetry continued developing as a strong oral tradition as it is today in Eastern Europe and Latin America. And it was a tradition in our country into the sixties with troubadour poets like Bly and Ginsberg when we, the academics, then took it into the classroom introducing words like "explication" and "scansion," onto the written pages of dissertations and theses...where people now needed the written page for comment and criticism. Criticism became a very big byproduct and in fact developed its own market. Poetry has thrived on its oral tradition from the very beginning. That poetry

---

Poetry has thrived on its oral tradition from the very beginning. That poetry enjoys a strong oral tradition in Eastern Europe and in Latin America today is because the poet represents a truth, a silent truth...

But let me approach this topic from another angle. Coming from European tradition and sensibility the way I do, I was not at all certain why I was asked to read in Moscow along with Dylan and Bly. I felt a little hesitant about the invitation. I knew why Dylan and Bly were asked, they represented the old and new schools in poetry but I wasn't at all sure about why I was invited. When I posed the question to the President of the Soviet Writers Union, I was told that I was asked because I was one of the few young American poets who were writing on subjects of gravity. He said something after that that amused me. "Many of your generation are writing what we refer to as pimple-on-the-neck poetry…as though America needs to be invaded to understand suffering." That said it all to me. That poetry enjoys a very strong oral tradition in eastern Europe and Latin American countries today is because the poet represents a truth, a silent truth, often heard the loudest in the silence between the words…such that people would come together by the thousands to listen because the suffering was communal. The next day the poetry would be published in 100,000 copies and the following day it would be sold out to lines of people stringing along and around the street corners.

Many of your generation are writing what we [Russians] refer to as pimple-on-the-neck poetry – as though America needs to be invaded to know what suffering means.

There is the story about Neruda who was asked whether he could recite a certain poem of his and he said he couldn't because he didn't have that poem along and then spontaneously the crowd recited it aloud together. That is the power of oral tradition.

Troubadour: Robert Frost can be the subject of considerable contention depending on who you talk to. Few deny his general popularity but at the same time they often tend to diminish the glow—something that is easy to interpret as professional jealousy or sour grapes. Just where do you think Robert Frost stands among modern poets?

Ragan: Well first of all, Robert Frost enjoyed a long life. At the time when he was most popular there was another group of poets including the likes of TS Eliot, Allen Tate, and John Crowe Ransom who were the formalists also known as the new critics. The kind of poetry they were writing is what I sometimes call "Eliotic," a footnoted kind of poetry that so

7

required the reader to know his mythological allusions and symbolism that it left a huge portion of the population out of the mix because folks were just not going the take the time to attempt to decipher that kind poetry despite how celebrated it was. It left out the person who enjoyed rhyme and accessibility.

That was when Frost enjoyed great popularity because he was the common voice dealing with subjects of interest to the common person. He would deal with the moral landscape and his poems were internationally accessible. Even in Russia everyone talked about "Stopping by the Woods on a Snowy Evening." During that time Frost got very tired of how his poems were interpreted. There was a great deal of Freudian interpretation and criticism of poetry and what it meant. University criticism was taking over the field.

I still recall an essay Frost wrote about "Snowy Woods" where he said, Look, I was writing a long poem entitled "New Hampshire" and it was working…it was moving and I just decided to take a break. So I went to take a walk on the porch. It was just near dawn and I saw a sleigh going by towards the far woods – the neighbor's woods – with its bells ringing. I realized that this little break away from the other poem gave me a little rise and that as much as I wanted to enjoy this short moment with nature I still had words to write before I sleep…or miles to go before I sleep.

How many things have to happen to you before something occurs to you?

Frost didn't mind doing lead-ins to his poems. I do the same thing at times. The audience isn't sitting there with the poems in their grasp and it's difficult to absorb words and meaning even when the poetry is easily accessible. He became the popular poet he clearly was because he spoke the common language to the common person in words that crossed borders and were easily translated. He once said something that is on the surface simple but at the same time remarkable. It was, " How many things have to happen to you before something occurs to you? That was about the word, insight, that every poet wrote—or ought to—with insight. I think he really cared about that. He set the defining parameters for formal and free verse with his well known statement, "Writing free verse is like playing tennis with the net down." He also made enemies with his stand, something almost all poets sooner or later feel compelled to make.

Frost has influenced me because of the dramatics of his poetry. I remember as a young man listening to him deliver his poem at the Kennedy inauguration. At one point he was reading and there was a bit of a drizzle and a gust of wind came along and blew his papers away…and he continued delivering without a hitch. I loved that moment. It really influenced me about what a poet could and should be.

I have loved and written every kind of poetry and poets of every kind have had their influence on me.

I believe that if you can communicate well, you can win battles with words instead of fists.

Troubadour: …or die honorably trying!

A Commentary by Henry George Fischer

Some Thoughts about Rhyme

Since the readers and contributors of Troubadour obviously favor rhyme, it's hardly necessary to defend it. But it may be useful to remind ourselves of the ways in which rhyme strengthens a poem or, if misused, weakens it. Apart from the inherent pleasure of rhyme, its most conspicuous function is to effect a cadence, reinforcing the end of a line or stanza, and especially the end of the entire poem. Thus the sonnets of Shakespeare end resoundingly with a rhymed couplet. And when he uses blank verse in his plays, he employs couplets to lend conclusive impact to a scene:

> Hear it not, Duncan, for it is a knell
> That summons thee to heaven, or to hell.

Conversely, a poem will undoubtedly be weakened if rhyme is adopted at the outset only to be forsaken at the end. Nothing, after all, is so important as the ending. If anything, rhyme needs to grow firmer, more insistent, as it reaches that point. This is well illustrated by Matthew Arnold's "Dover Beach," which, even though it does not follow a fixed pattern of rhyme, is terminated by two successive rhymed couplets. And Coleridge's "Kubla Khan," as it reaches its conclusion, twice uses a triple rhyme:

> I would build that dome in air,
> That sunny dome, those caves of ice!
> And all who heard should see them there,
> And all should cry, Beware! Beware!
> Weave a circle round him thrice,
> And close your eyes with holy dread,
> For he on honeydew hath fed,
> And drunk the milk of Paradise

Coleridge's terminal lines are also recurrently reinforced by the a-b-b-a pattern known as chiasmus, a literary device that lends power to any kind of repetition. And in case you wonder if "paradise" is a perfect rhyme, it's only in this country that some pronounce the ending as "ize."

On page 30 of this issue you will find a particularly striking example of how rhyme can affect structure.

It has become fashionable to adopt "slant rhymes," which are defended because a certain amount of irregularity may be desirable: wide/night, wise/ice, of/enough, current/torrent. There is a danger in this, for such rhymes may become so slant as to be ineffective (sing/bang). And for the reason stated earlier, perfect rhymes are in any case preferable in the last lines of a poem. One type of slant rhyme that is probably well to avoid altogether is the "sight rhyme," which looks like a rhyme but is not—"love" and "prove," for example. Although it appears in the works of the most renowned poets, from Shakespeare to Shelly, it may seem unseemly for us lesser mortals to copy the minor imperfections of the great.

The most exasperating error is the identical rhyme, which is apt to insinuate itself when you're not looking. One example, recently noted in another publication, is "consensus" and "census." The master rhymer, Willard Espy, author of Words to Rhyme With, rightly declares such a rhyme to be no rhyme at all. It is allowed in French poetry, where it is regarded as "rime riche." But as far as English is concerned, only the device called chiasmus can possibly redeem it, as in the following quatrain, concerning light verse as opposed to verse that lacks meter and rhyme:

> The bells on our toes
> Will ring the defeat
> Of the lead in the feet
> Of the makers of prose

It hardly need be said that an unaccented suffix does not make for a satisfactory rhyme—even a "slant rhyme." And yet this obvious lapse is often to be seen in periodicals that have some use for formal verse.

Rhyme schemes are many—too many to discuss here. It might be sufficient to point out that if rhymes are too distantly separated; they may not be easily registered by the ear. And it should be kept in mind that rhyme is, in fact, addressed to the ear and not the eye. So it is undoubtedly a good idea to reread a poem aloud before deciding that it's ready for publication.

Henry George Fischer is Curator Emeritus of Egyptian Art at the Metropolitan Museum of Art in NYC. His poetry—light, often erudite and always ever so precise—has been included in The Lyric and Light journals as well as in Random House anthologies of light verse.

A Concession to Modernity and Freedom

First Things
John Woodrow Presley

Who knows how the sacred king dies—
netted in a bath, pushed from a height,
eaten in a soup, a staged chariot crash,
or bitten in the heel by a viper?

Not a living Roman historian
knows the means of olive production,
knows the range of the Balearic sling,
or knows how to cook mallows or lupin.

What breathing scholar has read by oil lamp
seen the mushroom shadow cast by the wick,
and known when He died or how long She reigned,
the five-leafed herb the flying salve will need?

What coffin holds Arthur,
how the unicorn got its tail,
what name Achilles took to hide among women,
why grass and tree were made before stars?

Or less, finally to see for himself
the spinning silver islands of the dead
will press the venomed quill
into the flesh of his own heel.

When the Night Comes Down
S.J. Welker

In my small town
When the night comes down
And the sky is filled with stars
The old men meet on empty streets
And count the passing cars

In my small town
When the night comes down
And the houses fill with light
The young girls cry their sweet good byes
To the boys who chase the night

In my small town
When the night comes down
And the evening shades are drawn
The prayers are said beside the bed
And all our fears are gone

And late at night
When my sleep is light
And the child in me is free
In my small town
When the night comes down
Is where I dream to be

ODE TO AN UNTUNED LYRE
Tatiana Retivov

for Joseph Brodsky, *ex anima*

I've kept it high and dry, beyond repair,
a broken driftwood carving on the shelf
untuned and overwrought as is my self,
covered with lacerations, wear and tear.
My muse is gone, and with him goes my voice
buried beneath the sinking city's arcs,   it
climbs the mildewed walls along St. Mark's,
shrieking *"hic sepultus..."* It has no choice
but let its chords entwine with weeping vine
and like the seven strings of a guitar
emit, *de profundis,* a plaintive bar
until it is less vocal than divine.

The river Styx is where I'd like to be,
swimming upstream against this you-ward pull
toward some Orphic idyll in which you'll
metamorphose to be--Euridyce,
while I, swift-footed Hermes by your side,
would guide you firmly through the asphodels,
bending your ear with winged words and spells,
keep you from hearkening, the breathless bride.
Ensconced in Orphic garments she would not
repeat the warning trembling on her lips.
Recite instead the catalogue of ships.
See how Charon emerges from the grot...

Or else, like some Alcestis on her throne,
I would aspire to give up my lyre,
(untuned though it may be and now unstrung)
give up my heart, my restive name undone,

no longer marking time to my own rhyme.
Survivor's guilt perhaps, I'd give you life.
Return you to the manger where your wife
and child remain bewildered and inclined
to weave and then unweave what for a song
has become history, legend and myth.
Let the more loving one be me, Iosif.
Here's one more for the road, and then anon.

For Emily Dickinson
Earl Carlton Huband

These plots of earth stir far below,
beneath the heart of the hill,
a ground where gravestones slowly grow
round one with time to kill.

The dissipating clouds drift by,
beyond the stone of the hill,
where one – at heart – cracks in reply,
reverberating – still.

Jane Eyre For Modern Readers
Gail White

My boss is an attractive man.
He touches me and my heart gives off static.
I 'd love to tame him and I think I can.
Who gives a damn what goes on in the attic?

I had one of those...
D. A. Prince

There's a garden centre dementia –
is it freesia amnesia
or gardenia schizophrenia? –
that turns this carnation nation
from delphinium delerium
and wisteria hysteria
to sub-tropic neurotics.
So we're suckers for yuccas
nurture African daisies like crazy
and go bananas for nicotianas.

But our summers are bummers –
no recessions for depressions –
unless there's no doubt it's drought.
So a gardener's song goes: I had one of those...

but it died.

Be Timid in the Tundra
Bruce E. Newling

If you should go where Esquimaux
And caribou reside,
Refrain from dares with polar bears,
From which it's wise to hide;
For polar bears are known to chew
On tender morsels such as you.

The Libertine's Liebestod
Joseph S. Salemi

Grand passion has gone out of style, thank God—
We now have brief connections that don't last.
The flesh impels us, like a sharpened prod,
To get right down to business, and work fast.

Romantic love-throes wreck the nerves and brain,
And turn life to a masochistic dance—
Should one go broke and crazy to maintain
An out-of-date tradition from Provence?

Better the quick and temporary link
Wherein erotic impulse is condensed;
Better the motel tryst, I tend to think,
Than Tristan's moans and Romeo's laments.

For after all, the whole thing's simply this;
A look, a touch, the *frisson* of a kiss.

Defer to Lordly Lions
Bruce E. Newling

If peradventure you should meet
A pride of lions on the street,
Then my advice is step aside –
Don't trifle with a lion's pride.

The Size of Things
J. D. Smith

Things get smaller as we age,
As verified when we return
To childhood's home—too small a stage,
Too cramped for anyone to learn

A mother tongue, a social grace,
To ride a bike, to add a sum,
But every place remains in place
And states it earthly firm *I am*:

A once-big desk at once-big school,
A shrunken church, a shrunken store,
An oceanic backyard pool
Diminished at its bluegrass shore.

So here our letters were addressed
Once we left for brighter lights,
Which we've since seen, and aren't impressed.
The old familiar smallness blights

The capitols of foreign lands,
Stunts their mountains, tames their wilds.
Repetition comprehends
Our making love and what it yields.

Such secrets as exist are bared,
And after eighty years are done
We're full of time and stand prepared
To meet the life to come, or none.

Dudley Do-Right Tries His Hand at Poetry
Joseph S. Salemi

If the shoe fits, wear it.

It's certainly a challenge, but why not?
I'm nothing if not daring and intrepid.
Whenever life has put me on the spot
I've shown the world my mettle isn't tepid.
Of course, I'll only write what's good and true
And what helps others, or supports the law—
I'll stand up for the old red, white and blue,
And never pen a line that's lewd or raw.
I'll steel myself with all my might and main,
To fight against the vulgar and the crass—
My antiseptic verse shall not contain
A thing to shock Missouri's middle class,
Or any word or phrase or trope or thought
That doesn't sound exactly as it ought.

Respect the Noble Gnu
Bruce E. Newling

It does not do to boo a gnu
A creature large and haughty;
The view of gnus regarding boos
Is that they're very naughty.
If you think booing gnus is fun,
It would be well if you can run.

In the Thirtieth Year
Diane Thiel

> *In the thirtieth year of life*
> *I took my heart to be my wife*
> —J.V. Cunningham

In the thirtieth year of life,
she took her heart to be a wife.

And as she turned her head at night
to quench the final candlelight,

the dreams that never crossed her lips
might have filled a thousand ships,

might have found a passage home,
and yet she sank them, stone by stone.

Geologic
Diane Thiel

A geologic second passed.
We waged a hundred thousand wars,
believing each to be the last –
our geologic second passed.

A new millenium – at last,
and deep within the planet's core,
another millisecond passed.
We wage a hundred thousand more.

21

On Leaving the Wood
Peter Hanke

The wood you have grown in has many colors
And shadows streaming through leaves from the sun,
Many noises and forces, many kinds of creatures,
Choices, chances, and dangers that you run.

Oaks towering over marsh and meadow, caves
Plunging to glowing water, starred skies,
Valleys, and hills, and rocks, it is a world
To watch and touch, to work, to judge and prize.

Your eye and foot have learned its traps and paths,
You take delight in its reversing moods,
Its great wings of air always pouring
And spreading from dark altitudes.

The body of the wood is always breathing,
Signals flashing, the moving moon changing,
Dreams crowding the edges of your passage
Along the years your memory is ranging.

The sun is somewhere always, as you journey
Through glades and thickets across the uneven ground
Or sleep in the rush of the storm, or wake to startle
The eyes of animals with your human sound.

But the time comes at last, as it came to those
Or many of those before you, when the wood
Seems the same, too long it seems the same,
Or living there seems harder than it should.

While briers and flies, lies, the whirling weather,
The tedious food and drink, take their toll,
Your malady may, its own specific, struggle
To overcome or undermine your soul.

You should not let it, for while you are wondering
Whether to leave the wood by your own will,
As many before you have wondered and left or not,
The wood, the ancient wood, is lovely still.

What you should do is turn to the wood again
With new eyes and let it be stranger.
Perhaps each year you should consider leaving
The wood by your will, despite the danger.

sweetness IS bigger or smaller than a line
J. B. Mulligan

Acquinas points out: "...it is odd to say
that sweetness is bigger or smaller than a line."
By which he means: comparisons are fine,
but keep your orange peel off the apple tree.
Tracing each good's originality
through root to seed, beyond...he always finds
one beneprimal cause, supreme, behind –
the fruits of which we savor as best we may.

But there's no strangeness in the thought: the way
that words can flower and concepts intertwine
is how I ape a massed reality –
and put my lips to God's. And what I bind
vaguely recalls the shapings that I see
hold all disparate truths for desperate clay

the ridges of the moon
J. B. Mulligan

Briefly, startled from sleep
as the bus shuddered up a hill,
she seemed, beside me, young –
but it was still

the woman who had sat
an hour ago, whose face
was nicked and creased, her life's
collisions traced

like the ridges of the moon.
But now, in sleep, the skin
had smoothed and plumped to a blurred,
reflective shine,

and I saw the shadows of
a past of snows and fires
in a distant, neighboring land.
A little later,

in the terminal, as she walked
quickly, erectly away,
I said goodbye to her back.
There was nothing to say.

Caught
Charles Rafferty

A small vibration in my palms was all
I wanted: bees inside a jelly jar,
wings attacking glass. I still recall
their fist-size song filling me with fear.
The snapping turtle from the drainage ditch
Took over my tank of angelfish. It fed
and grew, demanded more, became a touch
that terrified, muscled among the dead.
The mallard eggs I smuggled home refused
to hatch all month. I'd robbed a riverbank
only to learn their weight, the way they dozed
in a box of socks until they broke and stank.
Nothing I kept survived the way I thought,
the merciless ordeal of being caught.

City of Westminster
Ruth C. Holzer

Every time I had the chance
　　　　I'd take some of that paper
The City of Westminster purveyed,
　　　　To lay up stores for later.

Big Ben on each waxy sheet,
　　　　Though cheap and flimsy, without fail
It beat the stuff my landlord gave:
　　　　The *Evening Standard* on a nail.

Secret Agent
Henry George Fischer

Incognitized, he'll let none know
The hand he does not want to show,
No, not a finger. He is so
Disguised that not a single toe

Of what he stands for is perceived.
Like Burnham Wood he is beleaved;
Were he reproved, he'd be reprieved
By seeming not to have deceived.

Nor will *Who's Who* provide a key
To indicate that he is he,
For what he is alleged to be
Belies his own biography.

Yet he can't be dismissed, for he's
The very mist of mysteries.

Do Not Try to Rush a Rhino
Bruce E. Newling

With a rhino on the road
When you're riding on your bike,
If you use your horn to goad,
He will use his as a spike.

A Lesson in Comparative Zoology
Joseph S. Salemi

There is a strong filiation in the line
Of higher apes, and that which we call man:
The upright stance, articulated spine,
Bipedal locomotion. Students can
Observe resemblances in face and form,
The inner organs, dietary needs,
And even—though on this point there's a storm
Of hot dispute—behavior of the breeds.
The males are hierarchical, but mate
With any lissome female they can snare;
They move in packs, and do not tolerate
Dissent from groupthink, so one doesn't dare
Stir up a man or ape's profound emotions
On status, sex, or fixed communal notions.

Evolution's Triumph?
Don Miguel

In the midst of serenity
a numbing impulse occurs.
He starts and turns as though the urge
was audible and loud. What stirs
inside is neither demon nor
devil, just traces of a past
that dwell in inner shadow.
Survival at the very last
is not a matter of thoughtful
choices, of morals—good or ill.
The last to stand will heed the urge,
will do the unthinkable, kill!

Mirror, mirror
D. A. Prince

Caught in the half-light, you
could be quite something, a
moodier version of
Greta Garbo:
high defined cheekbones, that
brooding intensity –
quite the self-image you're
yearning to show.

Glare of a bare bulb, and –
God! There's a hag for you!
Scrawnily, owlishly
scowling and sad.
More like Miss Haversham
haunted and hollow-eyed,
crinkled and wrinkled
and clearly half-mad.

To Catalina

The perfect flower is rare indeed
Descendent of a golden seed
Which, kissed at night by moon and dew,
At dawn becomes the rose that's you.

In Search of Truth
Don Miguel

Somewhere in far-flung space
a star drifts aimlessly
uncertain of its place.
At times it restlessly
winks this way and then that—
not knowing which way's right
or where God hangs his hat—
hoping, praying it might
illumine something never
starlit or moonstruck blue,
something terse and clever
and...inarguably true.

Video Game
David Stephenson

It's like those pinball games we had before;
The lights and sounds are better, but there's still
A set of balls you bat around until
You miss a shot and don't have any more.
Adolescent boys make up the core
Of its small clientele. They slowly fill
Its box with quarters begged from Mom, and kill
Their idle hours running up the score.

I've more or less outgrown this sort of game.
The flash and racket don't do much for me
And I feel guilty tossing time away.
What's worse, you always end up with the same
Evocative result: eventually
The last ball always clatters out of play.

29

Octagon
Linda Bosson

She sits in the octagon tower,
Staring at shadows all day
And twisting her hair by the hour.
They have taken the windows away.
They have bricked up the arch of the door,
And the weeds have crept over the wall.
Her songs are not heard any more.
Her name is not spoken at all,
Though an old man once said, "I regret
That my love slipped away as I slept.
Her name was...her name...I forget."
And that night in the tower she wept.

Five Bikus in Search of a Hearing
Henry George Fischer

Like the ghost of something that's interred
At most you're hardly overheard.

You pack a wallop when you write,
But when it's unpacked, it shows no fight.

How can it happen that what you shout,
When put in print, has lost its clout?

How can it be that all your rage
Has turned to petulance on the page?

To you your voice seems clarion clear,
But if you have readers, can they hear?

Note: *Biku]* a haiku bisected by rhyme

An Abandoned Garden
Robert Crawford

By August I noticed a lack of care,
And now in September I feel the despair;
The rusting tools, the vanished rows,
Reveal an all too brief affair.

The hopeful beginning has come to a close
As a meeting place for sinister crows
And devious weeds planning for when
They'll make this a plot where anything goes.

What kind of errant husbandman
Would let it fall to field again?
I think I know, I've met a few:
A fine egalitarian—

The type of man, a touch askew,
Who holds the universal view,
"To everything, a heart be true,"
But saves desertion just for you.

I Must Climb Down
Maureen Cannon

I must climb down from my merry-go-round
For the moment, the better to see
The way it looks from my place on the ground,
Spinning crazily by without me.

I must catch sight of my riderless horse
As he chases his tail in the sun.
I may climb back (finding reasons, of course).
Or stay where I am, finding none.

Westhof
M.A. Schaffner

The Wagner Ranch has stood a hundred years.
Four rooms down and a loft. Johnny Kahlich,
the restorer, shows off his Brangus steers,
then holds a palm of hand-cut nails – red, thick,
triangular. Shows the parlor, stenciled
by a man whose son fought for his homeland
in the Great War, but let himself get killed.
Today the Texans around me still blend

Plattdeutsch with cowboy. Aunt Ellenora
remembers the upright Pianola,
Saturdays nights, and the young folks' dances:
"All the farmers had piano rolls then
from ragtime to 'Deutschland über alles.' "
They don't know what uniform he died in.

The Forsaken One
Bryon Howell

I'm sorry I can't sing you lullabies,
or be a member of the PTA,
or wipe the tears of life out of your eyes –
when you are down, add sunshine to your day.
I thought I was so ready for all this,
An honor which should never be forlorn;
You'll never come to know my goodnight kiss –
you had to die before you could be born.
I'm sorry I can't bring you to the store,
or take you to the Ringling Brothers show;
my own needs were too pressing to ignore –
I chose to end you, snuff you, let you go.
I'm sorry that I let you rise and fall...
you see, I'm not so selfish after all.

Endurance
Esther Cameron

Friend of my friends, let none think to disjoin
By telling tales, my thoughts from them or you;
Whatever wrong you did, or they may do,
I grieve for it, as for a fault of mine.
All faults are but the fractures of one being
Beneath the hammer of an angry foe,
Or else the echoes of one voice decreeing,
"In the world where you live, it must be so."
I will believe that all are as they seemed
In the holy mirror of the One Desire,
Even such as the martyrs might have dreamed
The living, from their sleep beyond the fire:
However Time those images betray,
I will believe these dead shall rise someday.

Muse
Michael P. McManus

When all the starry skies have come to pass,
And grave Atlas shrugs his world to the ground,
Because the morning green has left the grass,
And the village churches have lost their sound,
I know a kind of beauty will remain,
Wading a stream, wearing a summer dress,
Easy at night, or easy in the rain.
Now as then she has nothing to confess.
Yet years I've desired to be her priest,
Sitting in dark, her face a breath away.
In that black space where I gather the beast,
I give acquittal to myself and pray
For my body that trembles, and as such,
Covets the soul that it can never touch.

Mystery
Jim Dewitt

Slightly smoked,
a solitary cigarette
        standing in the sand –
poled monolith in miniature
begets the questions:
        Where is he who sucked?
        Or she who blew?
Did they tire of nicotine
and shout "I'm through!"
Perhaps they quelled their cravings,
felt so proud
and then in celebration
right out loud
they said:
        "as monument to Will
        we'll bury this with filter down
        for chancers-by to find,
        give them pause to wonder
        (if sound of mind)" –
So what kind of swearing-off
Has led to this tra-la-la-lee?
Why an interment illusory
for all of us to see...

That Double-Headed Candle Again
Louis Phillips

I burned my candle at both ends,
A studied eccentricity,
But Ah my foes! & oh my friends,
Sinning's better with electricity.

34

Rhyme
Henry George Fischer

While many feel that rhyme's a must,
It is discarded with disgust
By others. And it's clear each view
Depending on the case, is true:

Whereas the use of rhyme defines
And dignifies the poems we write,
It stigmatizes verse that's trite;
And that is why we say sometimes

To welcome it, or else to slight,
"The best of rhymes, the worst of rhymes."
Though it's not just the rhymes we mean
But all the words that intervene,

The painful poverty of which
May beggar rhymes that should enrich.

Peas, Please
Stephen Kopel

What are the odds
       of my pods lacking peas
after all those mornings
       down on my knees?

Yet, if their DNA's dapper
       and sticking to duty,
each lustrous green pearl
       will uncurl as a cutie.

Bliss
D. A. Prince

Bliss it is, long past dawn, to slumber on,
but to be truly snug is very Heaven.
Somewhere, outside, the world may bump along.
I might consider rising at eleven –
but *such* an effort, looking at the clock;
I'll turn the radio on – eventually.
I could…but no: why risk a nervous shock
by getting up to fetch a cup of tea?
"The world is too much with us" – poets can't
quite understand we don't all twitch and jump,
are happiest when undisturbed, and aren't
like wide-eyed kittens, more a tortoise lump
in hibernation's shell, a *dèja vu* way,
tucked tight beneath some teens of togs of duvet.

Midnight in the Snow
Laurie A. Jacobs

Its wild, fiery eyes aglow
An anger, till now, I did not know.
      Fresh upon the midnight air—
They cast upon the melting snow.

Its wings, they swoop and carry away
All fragile smiles of the day;
      Provoked by emptiness inside,
And each time leaves a different way.

Remorse for burdens I should not bear;
Haunted by memories of deep despair,
      A truth, which, each day depletes
My heart, which carries a cold night air.

Dancing Moon
Laurie A Jacobs

The nights pass,
Awaiting creation
Of a new day
And sun's fascination.

The moon dances
Over my head;
Suffocating my mind
Weaving thy thread.

Of waking moments
In despair,
And how the heart
Shall soon repair.

Still, the nights pass,
Awaiting creation
Of a new day
And sun's fascination.

Elpenor in Hades
Rhina P. Espaillat

The gods don't give a rat's ass for my sort.
They keep track of their bastard kin—oh yes,
Theseus and Hercules—but as for us,
we're just an afterthought.

The least and youngest of Odysseus' crew,
I broke my neck after a drunken fall.
And good enough: I'm not heroic, tall,
a prince. What else is new?

Local News
David Stephenson

The anchors greet us. Pictures fill the screen.
They open with a murder or a fire
And cut to a reporter on the scene

Who's snagged a cop. The questions are routine.
He darkly hints that it was done for hire.
The anchors banter. Pictures fill the screen.

Somewhere, some sort of meeting had convened.
An angry spokesman calls someone a liar.
The dutiful reporter on the scene

Says thanks. The crack investigative team
Exposes some new scam with righteous ire.
The anchors scowl. New pictures fill the screen:

Commercials, lotto numbers. Does this mean
That I slept through the baseball scores? I tire
Of all of these reporters, all these scenes

Boiled down to fit this time-restricted scheme,
This flattened fast-paced universe entire
Revealed through pictures flashing on the screen,
Filled with reporters, begging to be seen.

Sonnet for Three Cats
Simon Hunt

Bedtime—we let slip these cats of mayhem
that slink between feet and scratch up the night.
They chase and yowl and pull in tufts the hairs
of their partners in criminal damage.
Fortunate mornings we escape bedlam,
assess their work. Worse nights, by claw and bite
we're summoned from dreams to awful tearings.
Come four there's no predicting the carnage.
We kid ourselves, my wife and me, that we
keep cats because they are so clean. That's Will
now—pulling houseplants down. His small colleague?
She's preparing an armchair for the kill.
But the third, tonight's darling, lies curled, warm;
together she and I wait out the storm.

Final Act
John Schmidt

At last we realize it was no act at all.
Why does it take us to be gone
to know we love? Does the glare
of lights on stage stop the moment,
and cause the curtain to be drawn?
Because I can't remember lines
well enough to play a role today,
I only know your love in loss,
The star-struck night of yesterday.

Changing on Sunday
Michael S. Smith

I watch you slip on your best Sunday dress,
Your jewelry and beads ready to work
Their magic, hair and makeup nothing less
Than perfect. You say, "I'm off." You don't flirt.

I busy myself while you are away
And think about anything but what you
Are doing there. It pains me, naturally,
To watch you leave, the wife I thought I knew.

Think about it. We ridiculed nonsense
Together, worked hard years to get ahead,
And never questioned our staid common sense
Or rational virtue. And now its dead?

Your rosary worried me less than this,
Communion with another man at Mass.

On The Value of having The Last Days of Pompeii in One's Library
Louis Phillips

In the middle of the night I turn my light on
To read the works of Edward Bulwer-Lytton.
4 minutes later (how those slow minutes creep!)
I switch off the light & fall back to sleep.

April
Douglas K. Currier

The cruelest month, my ass, I have seen worse.
Septembers with no burning piles of leaves;
January so cold, the blood believes
there is no love, no month unfit to curse.

February – so helpless, hard and terse.
And March, that flirt – inconstant, endless tease.
July, a tired smile, tries hard to please.
October masks its loathing – plucks your purse.

I've suffered damage in each time of year.
By season, month, and day, I've been betrayed.
The date, the time, each phase has nodded by,

has shuffled, snuffled, beckoned back a tear;
and I have listened, marked, and turned each page
of calendars, have understood the lie.

Lysistrata
Keith S. Petersen

You passive, women, will you never come?
—to this I mean, this rally that I've called.
Cry, if you must, to get away—then run!
To bawl is better than being balled.

We need to organize—not only here
but Sparta, too, and everywhere in Greece—
then teach our men; the message must be clear:
Make peace!—or never get another piece.

Inept
Douglas K. Currier

Shall I confess how often I have tried
to stop this hand, bind with some strong tether,
this thought that wanders freely, together
with poverty of vision, excess pride.

Or how, too late, I've labored to abide
by limitations in ugly weather,
imagination as cracked as leather
left in the sun – an old and salted hide.

Of love, know little more than how to lose;
of flesh, suspect no more than I can feel;
and life, in passing by has left me dumb

in every sense the colors of a bruise.
And still I write, and still contrive to steal
the music, and the lyre, and the drum.

I've Been Pondering Eternity Again
Jennifer Reeser

While I was still a child, at night I lay
in stillness on my bed, stubborn to see
the farthest vestige of eternity
until within my mind, day piled on day,
each second piled thereafter, soon gave way
to such paralyzing fear in me,
I'd countermand those thoughts impatiently –
knowing (in time) forever couldn't stay.
By seeking paradigms outside their moment,
I'd tried to force forever to successions
of hours, as children might mistake atonement
for nothing more than sorry introspections,
then turned my bedside candle off to sleep,
with full faith that its lightlessness would keep.

Pedagogy Blues
John Schmidt

I'm tired of being a peddler of dreams.
Not dealing in drugs and not what it seems,
putting children on stars that pass in the night,
filling fireflies in jars just to make light.
I'm tired of casting my pearls before swine,
pretending peanuts are gems and water is wine,
looking for rainbows when nothing is there,
hearts – made for love – that simply don't care.

Serenade
Dan Campion

I slicked a bit of pomade on,
But, girl, don't plan to swoon;
His forehead's an accordion,
His nose a bass bassoon.
Bix Beiderbecke, this poem is not
Nor smooth Cab Calloway –
But put a nickel in his slot
And homegrown jazz will play.
I mean, he's got a raggy beat,
With brushes on the snare,
And clarinets and tapping feet,
And saxophones that blare.
You say his wall of sound falls flat?
I warned you (see line 2)
This one-man band smiles in his hat
And leaves the tune to you.

A Winged Word from Wilhelm Busch
Henry George Fischer

Vater werden ist nicht schwer;
Vater sein, dagegen, sehr!

Becoming a father's easy, but
To be one is, conversely, not!

Yet if it's hard for Wilhelm, how
Much more it is for Wilhelm's frau!

At the Senior Citizen Center
Nancy King

He walks into the room
And my heart skips a beat,
It does a neat little pit-a-pat.
I'm thinking, *Isn't love great*
And oh so romantic,
And all such junk as that.

The time rolls around
For my yearly physical;
No problem, I'm healthy as a horse.
But the Doc hears a sound
That isn't quite right
So he orders more testing, of course.

After an EKG,
An echogram
And a lecture on food consumption,
I learn that skipping beats
Doesn't signify love—
It's merely a physical malfunction.

A Witness Bird
Henry J. Mudlaff

Black as my feathers shone her hair,
The woman lingering in despair.
I watched her there on woodland floor,
On fallen log she sat, heartsore.
What held her mind in thought so deep
That made her pause, then made her weep?
Despondently, unknowingly,
She shared her complex world with me.
Unable to know, nor console,
That lonely, tearful, earth-bound soul,
From lofty limb I rose in flight
Still keeping her within my sight.
Then circling high on gentle breeze,
I left her there among the trees.

A Whole New You, Almost
David Hedges

You weigh the notion of a brainless clone
whose liver, kidney, bladder, lungs and heart
exist for you when you need a body part,
an eyeball here, a skin graft there, a bone
or two when yours go soft and it alone
provides a match: an instant à la carte
facsimile of you, though not as smart.
Your baby's born; its duplicates are grown
Like peas and corn, or raised like mindless sheep,
The goal, disease and injury control.
You watch, bemused, as human values shrink
And population takes a quantum leap.
The question now is how you weigh the soul
Of one who lives and breathes, but cannot think.

46

Metaphor
Midge Goldberg

Remember the lilac soap I bought up north,
When we were on that trip, oh, two months back?
The soap is almost gone. Dissolved, it sits
Forlorn, a sliver on the shower rack.
My knee still hurts from skiing that last day.
Romantically we tried a nighttime run;
My falling wasted moonlight on the snow.
I limped back to the car, adventure done.
The soap, the knee—in a story—would portend
Dissolving, breaking down: the lover's bane.
But in reality, the soap is—soap.
The knee is not a wrenching sign of pain.
We look for signs to tell us what to do,
The rub is that the looking makes them true.

Wheel Song
Jim Fisher

If you seek me, look towards
The ocean, out a hundred yards;
Where pelicans wheel into sun
End your search for I am one.

I am one flying out there
Who suddenly shifts in mid-air
And plunges into briny sea:
Lost below—O that is me.

That is me and this is I
From briny sea to bluest sky
I rise again, and into sun
Wheel until my wheel is run.

Talking Stick
Alfred Nichol

You're taken aback, I see—suspect a trick,
Or doubt your wits that witness eloquence
From a snapped-off, insect-riddled stick,

A scrap of wood without appeal to sense—
No rich elaborated curio.
But—closer—let us speak in confidence:

You sir, initiated contact. Oh,
A casual, unmindful act it was,
I'm sure. The action's taken, even so.

And I should judge a man by what he does,
Like wind or rain. Plainly the branch is broken.
I don't pay much attention to "because."

Kindling or rot, then, I can be outspoken.
I'll teach you what I know. Then you're dismissed.
The traveler's face turns ashen; ankles, oaken;

The stick is grafted on his knotted fist;
A nattering of wrinkled leaves is heard;
The dead wood keens; bark overlays a wrist...

What's sketched across the failing light is blurred:
A ghostly fallen limb, rooted in mist,
And, heavy on its stem, the bitter word.

Great Work!
Bruce Bennett

> "I got an A on my sonnet."
> > --overheard at a student reading

It's nice to be rewarded right away.
Pats on the back can keep you going strong.
I'm glad, my dear, your sonnet got an A.

You aced that test, and promptly got your pay.
That's the world's way. It's seldom ever wrong,
since, having been rewarded right away,

you're eager to perform another day,
go out and wow them, show them you belong.
Hey (you'll recall) my sonnet got an A,

I've got it down, I do my job okay,
darn well in fact. The big bell goes ding dong,
school lasts. Your been rewarded right away

which is the lesson. Oh at times you may
wonder if maybe something in the song
you put your heart in didn't deserve an A,

wasn't so hot perhaps. Well who's to say?
In time you'll give your own A's to the young.
It's nice to be rewarded right away.
I'm glad, my dear, your sonnet got an A.

What We Say
Bruce Bennett

She's doing pretty well for ninety-three.
It all depends on what you mean by well.
It's as it is, and as it has to be.

She used to say, "Your attitude's the key."
Her attitude today is hard to tell,
but still, she's doing well for ninety-three.

She hasn't lost her spunk. Mobility
's a problem; she complains that life is Hell,
but as it is, and as it has to be.

I hear it all each time I go for tea.
She thinks it isn't age; it's that she fell.
"You're doing pretty well for ninety-three,"

I tell her, but that's mostly said for me.
I've watched her dwindle, brittle as a shell.
That's as it is, and as it has to be,

and who knows for how long? We'll have to see.
Meanwhile, we chant our mantra as a spell:
She's doing pretty well for ninety-three.
It's as it is, and as it has to be.

Artisans
J. Weintraub

These words are my materials and tools.
I could never make a cabinet, bookcase, or chair
as you can – mutating wood to furniture – never dare
to use your lathes or saws, your squares or awls
(although I like the sounds of these words just the same)
to measure, join, to bevel, hew, chisel, or plane,
or with such patience press, massage those oils
into the pores and, layer-by-layer, the grain
of oak and cherry wood. I can just about change
a bulb; still, to shield them from the wear of time,
I, too, polish surfaces until they shine;
and shaping forms into something whole and new
are efforts, acts, we both can understand
as, on occasion, we step aside to view
our work, to wipe the sawdust from our hands.

On Track
Mildred J. Nash

Two woefully old folks dodder aboard Amtrak,
Carefully set themselves on the train's coast side
Of a Boston-New York route. By Providence
Out comes a picnic basket they unpack
Between them – food and cups and napkins plied
To complement the scenery against
Their wide-screen, real-life window. Across the aisle
A woman holds a phone she dials and dials.

I switch back to the two whose privacy
Resides amid so many worlds in motion;
They savor boatyards, inlets, birds, the quaintly
Painted stations as they feast. All done,
They drift on whistle riffs to nap briefly
Till New York sees them rise, the woman run.

No Accounting For This Love
Frank Miller

I cannot make our lives add up; there is no sum
to this subtraction, no real numbers, no neat rows,
now that I need them. The words too, will not come;
cadenced columns, sweet logic written in crisp prose
marching on immutable to a fixed and proven end.
You will not total, yet, to add you makes me whole.
No formula for friend, so much more than friend,
can enumerate or graph you, firmly fix your soul.
I cannot balance this account, I can never weigh
the worth of you. I've no proof but, have no doubt,
a sometime second spent with you is more than day
and seconds come in centuries when you are not about.
Then cast aside all logic, sum all in a single line,
this loving has no reason and bears no equals sign.

A Highbrow Ballade
Noam D. Plum

The use of rhyme and meter's obsolete.
Most magazines that publish poems adhere
To views that find verse falling into neat
Clean patterns dull, derivative, a mere
Game-playing, and their editors steer clear
Of anything so childishly perverse.
My poems are not the type that they revere.
Verse sounds more highbrow if it doesn't rhyme.

Elucidating their refined, elite,
And modern sensibilities, they sneer
That wielding rhyme and meter is a feat
Less for a poet than an engineer.
To them, set form's a shiny crass veneer.
There isn't much to which their more averse.
It's stodgy and offensive to the ear.
Verse sounds more highbrow if it doesn't rhyme.

"Your poems, sir, were received, and we entreat
You not to send us any more such queer,
Old-fashioned, drab, conventional, effete,
Stanzaic rot. It won't be published here.
We deal in modern poetry and we're
Not interested in your sing-song verse.
Who do you think you are, sir, Edward Lear?
Poems sound more highbrow if they do not rhyme."

Envoi
There's little doubt I chose the wrong career.
Prince, is there any occupation worse
Than writing formal poems? It would appear
Verse sounds more highbrow if its doesn't rhyme.

At the Musée d'Orsay
Gail White

The excuse for all these naked writhing marble
women is snakebite. Nineteenth century sculptors knew
how to squeeze sex out of a marble lemon!
The Academics had a trick or two

up their dark sleeves. Though the Impressionists
are just around the corner, they'll go on
heaping up naked Venuses and nymphs…
Lust lingers after theory is long gone.

Cabanel's Venus, amorously nude,
lolls, peeking upward, on a shelf of foam.
A centaur strikes a staggered attitude
as bare-bum nymphs go spiralling toward home.

These pretty pink flesh pyramids don't prove
a thing – no wonder that they all caved in.
But that damned glass carbuncle at the Louvre
can make me long for Cabanel again.

Bathrooms
Elisabeth Kuhn

The condo I just bought has two. Some houses
had three. What to do with them all? Use one?
Turn the others into extra closets?
Reserve one for guests? There are none
I'd invite. I talk too much to too
many people all day. On conference
weekends I have to talk Sundays too,
and when I close my door, I want silence.

Back home we were seven. Our bathroom the only
room we could lock in a house without keys.
We'd sit, read, dream, alone, not lonely,
until testy banging disturbed our peace.
Then we'd sigh, flush, put down our text,
and turn our sanctuary over to the next.

The State of American Poetry
Don Miguel

Far distant from this pristine place,
where men are great by right of birth,
there dwells a soul who suffers much
who neither knows nor asks his worth.
In deprivation hear him sing
of untold misery to pass,
while we such smug, pretentious things
pen odes to pimples on our ass.

The Modern Ajax
Max Gutmann

> *The hero halts and his associates waits.*
> — Pope's *Iliad*, Book XII

It doesn't seem quite kosher, to be candid.
The legalistic circumspection grates.
Whatever happened, pray, to "single-handed?"
The hero halts and his associates waits?

I grant you that a hero might have mates,
Compatriots with whom he's sailed and landed,
But this cavorting with "associ-ates,"
It doesn't seem quite kosher, to be candid.

The man's credentials ought to be demanded.
A hero who so baldly hesitates?
It's far too cautious, far too even-handed.
The legalistic circumspection grates.

It isn't what the contract stipulates.
When was the job description countermanded?
The time was, heroes had much firmer traits;
What ever happened, pray, to "single-handed?"

I see, alas, the sands of time have sanded
Our hero down. The way he abdicates
His role strikes me as almost underhanded:
The hero halts and his associates waits.

Unable to subscribe to any canned id-
Eology, nor trusting to the Fates
Not to disperse in air and leave him stranded,
The hero halts and his associates waits.
It doesn't seem quite kosher.

Yoyo Ma's Music Garden
Dorothy Winslow Wright

> *"Here we will sit and let the sounds of music
> Creep in our ears."*   William Shakespeare

Yo-Yo Ma, in soft blue Oxford shirt,
sits among the lilacs playing Bach.
The Cello Suite vies with meadowlark
posing on the fence. An extrovert,
the gregarious, singing, yellow-breasted flirt
ignores his guest: he is the patriarch
of grassy field. Yo-Yo, his arm in arc
of lyric grace, continues sylvan concert.

He dreams of music gardens, the melodies
of masters woven into winding trails
dignified with towering oaks, the power
of crescendos in Beethoven's symphonies;
the lento calm of quiet pond, the cattails
chocolate soft, blending with the flowers.

What We Spend in Getting There
Richard Wakefield

He found a logging road, unused and rough
with ruts eroded deep by runoff, blocked
where slides had torn across, but good enough
for one who wasn't hurried. And so he walked
its zigzag contours, let it lead him through
the second-growth now grown so high it might
have been primeval, though peering deep into
the undergrowth he now and then caught sight
of stumps as wide across as he was tall
and notched from springboards high above the ground
as he could reach. But he was glad for all
he had that day, these woods, the road he'd found,
and didn't let the loss of something more
weigh on his heart. Some miles on he came
to where a ridge sheered off. There lay before
him then a view that might have been the same
as someone there ten thousand years ago
had seen, the distant mountains glacier-crowned,
the forested horizon. Far below
a river without dams or bridges wound
its gleaming length, reflecting noonday sun.
He didn't have a camera, but learned
the scene by heart, a memory of one
unspoiled and hard-won hour, before he turned
the way that he had come. That night he told
his wife he wished together they could climb
to see what he had seen, to have and hold
between them something out of change and time.
Another summer came. He heard the road
was smoothed and paved, and not for logging but
for cars, and so he took his wife and showed
her where he'd been in hopes that she'd feel what
he'd felt. She said she liked the view. She said

it was as lovely as a picture. So.
A half an hour's easy drive had led
them here, an easy half an hour to go
where he had spent a long and sweaty day
afoot. And yet the air-conditioned ride
revealed less than had the harder way,
a way that he and she could not retrace.
He saw that part of being anywhere,
the better part, is nothing in the place
itself, but what we spend in getting there.

Negations
Rhina P. Espaillat

Sermons the seasons preach that never quite,
and yet almost persuade, almost deceive—
migrations, the fidelity of light,
those steady habits—want you to believe;

as if the mockingbird set out to say
one thing, but changed its tune and took it back,
as if the wind crossing the pond half way
lifted its sequined veil to show the black,

as if your days were plates of summer fruit
that you may wash and quarter, core and pare
for guests, until you notice they've gone mute,
gone home for good, if they were ever there.

Exceptions
Carol Hamilton

My mother was an English teacher.
     She sometimes broke the rules.
We, her children teased and laughed at her,
     The department head in a public school.

Today I dashed off e-mails like a fool,
     Put dashes and dots and my sentences blur,
'Till my readers say in ridicule,
     "Her mother was an English teacher."

"By that I do not mean to infer,"
     I reply, "that her words were elegant, cool,
For when she was overcome with fervor,
     She sometimes broke the rules."

She'd act out Shakespeare with leer and mewl,
     Do Robert Burns with a Scottish burr,
Never acknowledged our ridicule
     As we teased and laughed at her.

"I'm on vacation," she'd say with hauteur,
     "And grammar, you know, is only a tool.
Being slavish to it is too immature
     For the department head in a public school."

So I dash off this flurry of words and pray you'll
     Forgive how I've come to maim and massacre
The syntax, the laws. I'll take my place on the dunce's stool.
     What a lover of language and connoisseur
          My mother was!

Newton's First Law
Peggy Gwynn

What's resting is content to lie at rest,
but know a flame flows on the mountainside
and moving matter tends upon a quest.

Where countless continental shores suggest
immutability, sheltered cities bide.
What's resting is content to lie at rest.

Rains pound forsaken towns all moss-obsessed,
weeds frill on fragment earth, heir eagles glide
and moving matter tends upon a quest.

Apples dry slowly in a pantry chest.
A temperate man will hold his dreams inside.
What's resting is content to lie at rest.

Persistent sparrows weave the tweedy nest,
huntsmen frolic and freighters slash the tide.
A moving matter tends upon a quest.

Arrestless fêtes flare gently on the crest,
illumine the ways of the tried and yet untried;
what's resting is content to lie at rest
and moving matter tends upon a quest.

Song of Life
Newton Miner

It is no fantasy that comes at dawn
To shake you from the voyages of sleep.
Out of the tunnels of ancestral dark
A baffled beast comes howling in a blind
Search to shape a meaning for his kind.

Meaning was not intended. Nor was life.
A random, eager fusion in the blaze
Has brought us to this consciousness by day.
But what we gain by day we lose by night,
As entropy encroaches on the light.

No one can tell you what the darkness means,
And the multiple interpretations of
Light are vanity. Then let us bring
One more interpretation that will show
The blessing of existence as we go.

Let it be joy, as freshing forth of dawn
And ever-varied rising of the moon
Are of themselves life's affirmative.
Let meaning be the self-sufficing sun
Glad in a war he knows cannot be won.

And let it be a huge, unending hush
As, after the bauble sun, impress of night
Reminds us that the very essence of
Joy is brevity. And let us sing
In triumph for the life of everything.

Old Photograph
David Stephenson

I bought this dresser at an antique store—
Though it's not antique, it's just second-hand—
And found this photo in the middle drawer.
It must be old. The bell-hop suit the man
Is wearing has been out of style for years;
Likewise, the woman's jungle flower dress
Looks like it's from a Sputnik-era Sears.
I call them Uncle Bub and Auntie Bess.

There is no birthday cake or Christmas tree,
No writing on the back to indicate
What it once meant, what vanished memory
It served, before the bumbling hand of fate
Delivered it to me, a token from
The long blue tunnel of oblivion.

On Not Thinking About Elephants
Noam D. Plum

I want to learn to meditate.
I'm told I'll reach a higher state
of consciousness, and heightening
could be, I think, a real good thing,
so every morning, if I don't sleep late,

I focus on the gentle flow
of air, my breath. To get to know
my inner rhythm, I sit still
and let breaths glide just as they will
—or that's the way it's supposed to go.

But I can't seem to think about
the rhythm of my breath without
affecting it. I realize
the moment that I close my eyes,
I'm pulling deep breaths in and pushing out,

exactly what I'm *not* to do.
And when I get determined to
be more relaxed and not to force
the breath, I stop. But then, of course,
I feel my whole complexion turning blue.

Still, I intend to persevere
and someday master steering clear
of those dual foes of meditation,
the false, forced breath and suffocation.
Till then, my consciousness is stuck down here.

Shadow
Vicki Stringer

I walk on the cobbled terrace
to get to the screen door.
My shadow leads the way,
a creature on the floor—
the hair on the tiles snaking
like one of those ink-blot tests—
a Gorgon in the making.
The neck bizarrely rests
between the shoulders askew;
the arms are like melting wings
of Icarus as he flew.
Below the knees are stilts,
and I cannot find the feet,
cut off somehow in the place
where the shadow and sunlight meet.

And I wonder...

On the street when people pass by
with the usual pleasantry,
some look me straight in the eye
and see "the real me."
But others, with eyes on the ground,
much to my regret
see only my shadow—of course
what you see is what you get.

Old Song
Julia Thomas Hu

An ancient song in me has not yet died.
I hear it although faded now and tired
by life's defeats and loss of things desired.
Its notes embrace me like an evening tide.

It has been decades since I was a child
first listening to the tentative refrain
that would repeat throughout both joy and pain   .
a melody to calm a heart so wild.

The days are shorter, but my life is long.
I miss the people who left years ago,
and although others call on me, I know
that none can ease me like this faithful song.

Old song, you must have heard that we're the same.
Before I'm gone just whisper me your name.

Typical
B. D. Love

This world of toil and turmoil bends our backs—
again, the usual humiliations
burden the spirit till it nearly breaks
as the flesh goes through its withering contortions.

A man I know stands half his former size.
He never met his dreams and now he waits.
Failure dilutes another colleague's eyes.
It's only emptiness he contemplates.

My own life sometimesseems to run this way,
toward a typical oblivion:
nothing ahead that's worth a prophecy.
Nothing behind except for what is gone.

A sparrow builds a nest outside my door.
I try to think of what she's building for.

Leaving the Bittersweet
Rhina P. Espaillat

Vines so deep-rooted they outwit the frost
illuminate this page, the garden's text
of dormant shrubs whose script of twigs, crisscrossed
against each other and the sky, seems vexed
and jeweled by coils of red and saffron flowers.
Look how trees wear, along their blackened trunks,
rubrics of bloom, as in some Book of Hours
winter borrows the fantasies of monks.
Duty would have it gone, would pull it out
again, again, to keep the garden bare
in its bare season; but whose hand can rout
what rises from the dark to bless the air,
whatever Word such blossoming would mar?
Or can one follow metaphor too far?

Sage Advice
John Schmidt

Franklin said that fish and house guests
in just three days smelled bad to him
(I suppose unless they take a bath
or, in fishes' case, resume their swim).
Ergo, let's make our meetings short
not cloyed with what to do or say,
no need to languish to the bitter end
and watch the best of friendships fray.
I suspect that well-timed visits
are as much a metaphor of life—
to make most of moments then depart,
enjoy the rose, eschew its strife.

Time is not Always a Healer
David Hovan Check

The years move swiftly by us,
Leaving a void of discontent.
Success is spelled with a dollar sign,
The meaning of life being twisted and bent.
Misguided thoughts of devotion and trust;
Pneumonic patriots stand in the rain
And keep their faith in deceitful men
(Who shed no tears and feel no pain)
While plucking salt from the endless sea,
Grain by grain without wondering why,
And passing the harvest to overlords,
Who with it replenish the ocean's supply.
   O, perhaps someday they'll notice
   That the main will never dry,
   And stop inertly watching
   Their dead fathers slowly die.

Declan
B.D. Love

You're slowing down these days. Your old back curves.
The muscles shrink beneath the sagging skin.
It's no surprise. Such is the way time carves
the marble block of life. We all begin

solid and sharp, and end a pile of sand.
But I recall the eight-week-old that cried
and yelped beside the freeway fence. Abandoned.
I could have left you there, but I, afraid

to let a random dog inside my life
and more afraid to feed you to the cars,
bent down to snatch you up and make you safe.
You burrowed hard into my cradling arms.

I somehow drove you home, and you, once fed
surveyed your turf, then bit me so I bled.

On the Border
Carol Hamilton

Touch again my mother face, oh child.
I cannot cross this frontier to the past.
The day to day is lost, defiled

by my own way of looking Janus-faced,
not seeing glinted hair in morning light.
My sieved attention never made that moment last.

I slumbered in my case. Oh, wake, Snow White!
Attend what sidles past. It will be lost
where every flower closes in the night.

I shout and tell myself I'll rue the cost,
but my ears then are closed to my voice now.
She does not know how much I've lost.

So take my hand. We'll leave the crowd.
I promise I will listen. Teach me how.

Misses
John Schmidt

The road I never traveled,
the book I never read,
the deed I never finished
for the one I did instead,
a warm face I turned away,
the faithful friend I never met,
when I am old alone and blue
will be ones I won't forget.

Heart Like Glass
Katherine Brueck

Like broken glass, my heart jags skin all day,
Sadly picks up the nerve, presses the vein.
The blood pumps outrageously: I lay
My raised hopes down; I forfeit all dreams, as pain
Sings in whispers to the trumpets of time.
Longing lifts my bones, stretches my sides
Until I see joy from afar: a mirage or a mime.
When I walk I bruise, when I stride
I stumble. I fall in the dust of my love, never fed.
I seek a pill, a potion, an elixir, a cure:
I reach for a hand, a face, a hair of the head.
I grab the air: nothing, no one—too pure.
When will the eery path disappear? When will I
Awaken, spell gone, eager to live—then to die?

Villanelle for Political Pep-Rallies
Liz Robbins

Growing backwards, more childish by the day,
the governor's voice is young and amplified
while the American crowd shouts, "Hooray!'

At this political gathering, he'll say
his opponent has been telling them lies
growing backwards, more childish by the day,

and bowing his head, will ask them to pray
for all the votes their money can buy
while the American crowd shouts, "Hooray!"

(They've thrown responsibility away
like children, although each would deny
growing backwards, more childish by the day.)

Listen to the governor's boastful bray
(all the promises his stalwarts devised)
while the American crowd shouts, "Hooray!"

He says, "Don't let the votes fall where they may!"
He knows how fidelity can die:
growing backwards, more childish by the day...
while the American crowd shouts, "Hooray!"

The Tower of London Speaks
Don Miguel

A poet who is never read
might just as well be here
with any soul of yesteryear
who – *bearing* – lost his **head**.

To wit, a wife who bore no heir,
to wit, a man who brooked no lie…
and thus a bard who, by and by,
bred cryptic words—for he'd not dare

stick-out his neck for all to see—
voilà, lost his…summarily.

Cosmos
Burt Porter

I once went to the house of one whose mind
Had broken long before she'd finally died.
All that kept her going was her pride;
She lived for years alone and nearly blind
In a small world her madness had designed.
In delicate arrangements, she had tried
With twigs and string and eggshells to provide
For some strange fate her madness had divined.

The mice that knew no other world well might
Have thought (suppose they were intelligent)
That all was in accordance with hard laws
To be hypothesized and proven right.
The proof they could not find they would invent;
Intelligence demands there be a cause.

NTC 1957
Glover Davis

Stripped to the waist we moved between two lines
of corpsmen, needles glinting in their fists.
They plunged them in tattoos and flowering vines,
blocked letters, snakes uncoiling toward pale wrists.
My blank arms throbbed then rose like poisoned dough
before I made it halfway down this gauntlet.
A needle tip balanced a drop of snow
where the light burned, the needle long and wet
along the shaft where something dripped and horse
blood spotted it with rust. A corpsman raised
it over us like a truncated cross.
A recruit wobbled to the floor, as dazed
as any drunk. His white cheek pressed blue tiles.
After the smelling salts he shuffled through
the line again past trays of empty vials
whose fluids circulated near the blue,
black bruises of our arms' insulted skins.
They would inoculate us in an hour
against microbes millennia would spin
into our blood or brains where they might flower.
We pulled on white T-shirts and jumpers, lined
up in the yard outside, invulnerable
to some diseases, little else. We were blind
almost in the hot light flooding a gull
streaked courtyard white and washing over boots.
Even a gentle wind would nauseate.
Only time's febrile passage would commute
the burning, sluice the poisons with our sweat.

Family Mythology
Arlette Lees Baker

My boyhood hero was my Uncle Mick
who joined The Force and swung a mighty stick
and gave me smokes behind the backyard shed
caught thieves and murderers and shot them dead
to spare the honest citizens the pain
of trials, acquittals, catching them again.
He gave us rascals all his pocket change
and took us big shots to the shooting range.
Of course, the barroom beer was free at night
for cops who kept the city running right.
Hell's meanest *mutha* couldn't make him blink
but Irish music made him cry, I think.
He must have been the biggest toughest one
to chew them bullets when he ate that gun.

The Murphys' Rooster
Arlette Lees Baker

He's not a bird of melody or blithe
and should he sing for supper he would starve.
A lark invites the ear, but he the knife –
a rusty throat I'd rather twist or carve.

This fowl is on Viagra, it is clear –
he's over-sexed, incestuous and proud.
I plug my ears and down a calming beer
and still his concupiscence is too loud.

He crows before the sun at 3 or 4
when I am cuddled in my feather bed.
It's obvious the fool has lost his score,
yet dreams of show biz flutter through his head.

While he rehearses Grease and Camelot
I read my recipes and grease the pot.

Requiem in Smoke
For R.B. 1941-1998
Arlette Lees Baker

He'd strike a match against his shoe
and Bogey up a smoke,
shake up some change to score a pack
when he was cold and broke.

He viewed the shaft as Freudian,
the cinder as a jewel,
and with his rakish hat a-tilt
his stance was so damn cool.

The purple silk that floated up
dissolved and blew away,
seductive as the swirl of veils
that fell from Salome.

Like Dashiell Hammett's sleuth he lived
for nicotine and tar,
for saxophones and slinky jazz
just like a movie star.

At midnight in the alleyway
I sometimes see him there,
gone past the neon exit light
for one short drag of air.

Relics
Glover Davis

We pushed through heavy doors, moved down a hall
to a room lit by candles in a bank
of jars flickering tongues against the wall.
A mural where an avid shadow drank
St. Michael's double sword was bordered blue
on the coarse, white wash. The dyes the Indians made
from berries, leaves, egg yolks, retained a hue
as vivid then as when a Spaniard strayed
into this valley marking trails with stones
and the slashed trunks of California oaks.
Beneath the chancel lie the mouldering bones
of priest and soldier but the wind evokes,
some say, the slaughtered warriors buried near.
Wind moaning through high arches in the fall
creates the only semblance one might hear
of voices blocked by these adobe walls.
But Indian artists daubing Spanish blades
which reddened as they dried, preferred the vault
of blue outside, the vivid oaks, the shades
of gold, wild grasses rippled where the fault
lines crack the sacred earth. But we have come
to view these walls as though they framed a past
that never was. We do not see the foam
along the bridles and the lips. We'll cast
our coins into a wishing well outside.
We'll soon begin to blur and cancel much
of what we've seen and felt on the long ride
home, forgetting lives we cannot touch.

Fashion Note
Esther Cameron

One thing I sort of miss is ash-blond hair,
Or any of the other shades of mouse –
Grounds for complaint if it was yours to wear,
But like the shingles of a Cape Cod house
Or wave-smooth driftwood, comforting to see.
Its unemphatic plainness lets you trace,
As in good black-and-white photography,
Whatever was of interest in a face.
A fine-drawn eyelid, or a firm-set chin
Did not depend on polychrome to please,
And often the mute tones of hair and skin
Made up unique, elusive harmonies.
Now everyone flaunts forth in gold and red,
You see the hair, but not so much the head.

Revisiting Mr. Bartley's Burger Cottage
Deborah Warren

> *..they toil not, neither do they spin...*
> *Therefore take no thought, saying,*
> *What shall we eat?* —*Matthew VI: 28-31*

College-clever once, I never thought
how something reached my table: It was there,
with mustard, ketchup, onion rings—a hot
baconburger. Well, what did I care
how Mr. Bartley got his beef? I knew
important things; I was too bright
for detail. Maybe Bartley took a crew
and raided the kine of Helios every night.

Ask me today. Today I watched him getting
two vast vans of meat unloaded. Or
ask Mr. Bartley—crimson, white-haired, sweating—
just to sit—to toil not—to ignore
his spoiling beef and chat till he's revealed
such details to a lily of the field.

Portrait of a Grande Dame
Joseph S. Salemi

You've only one requirement for guests:
That they be charming in some novel way—
Dish out *bon mots*, light banter, risqué jests,
Or pose in youthful beauty by a tray
Of hot *hors d'oeuvres*. A liberal attitude
Governs your thoughts. You always seek to be
The mirror of an urbane latitude
Whose impulse, uninhibited and free,
Gives you those arms spread wide to greet a friend;
The broad sweep of your animated smile;
Those lavish gestures with which you extend
Your bounty in an open-handed style.

I must ask, though the question's unrefined,
Why does your world seem shrunken and confined?

First Death
Gail White

> *"Cain rose up against Abel, his brother,
> and slew him."*

When the blow fell, I laid it on the line:
"You were a lousy father. You neglected
them all. Our eldest was a good boy. He
wanted to love you. Why was he rejected?"

He only said, "I was preoccupied.
We were evicted – you know. I was making
a living. And I mourn the one who died.
Why waste grief on the other one for breaking

the Law?" That's men for you. As if I cared
about the Law. I would have broken thirty
laws to save Cain. He didn't know men died
if they were pushed a little. That was God's dirty

secret – we would die and not know when.
I'm out of his conspiracy with men.

Crossbred Vine
Ed Wier

The seed of death was planted at my birth,
And side by side with life the roots entwined;
This crossbred vine now covers all the earth,
With fruits of juicy pulp and bitter rind.
Theses seasoned twins of every mother's womb,
Each reaching for the unfamiliar ground;
The arms that rock us in our cradled tomb,
Will also drive us from the flesh we've found.
And now my time is coming o a close,
Will end with certainty I've never known.
I'll soon be done with all I can suppose,
To leave as I once entered here, alone.
When such a fate awaits, why do we stay,
And seek to sift the going from the way.

Missing My Calling
Ed Wier

The morning thunder spills across the plain,
Like sausage searing in a frying pan.
The woods are glowing with a hiss of rain,
Like weakened whispers of a dying man.
The light is lazy on the dripping leaves,
Like dusk, now lost and wandered up too soon.
The air is heavy with a hazy breeze,
That has no business in the afternoon.
The clouds are creeping shades of stringy gray,
Like cotton wet and stretched above the green.
Delivered on this day, a bland bouquet,
Of fresh-cut thoughts against a sagging scene.
I lie here listening in a twisted heap,
As something calls, but I go back to sleep.

The Organ Grinder's Monkey
Jan D. Hodge

The organ grinder always calls the tune.
Nutcracker is her special favorite.
The monkey knows whenever she renders it
that he must dance and clap his hands and beg
a pittance from the jeering crowd. His leg
tugs at the silver chain as he extends
the cup he cannot think his own, pretends
not to notice how much he is denied
by this. What does a monkey know of pride?
He answers only to his mistress' will,
keeping his hurting heart's own secret, till
she yanks his chain, shelves him for the night,
and counts the taking she assumes by right.
The organ grinder--she always calls the tune.

Hieroglyphics Gone…
Wally Kennicutt

Proud and ancient Egypt's knowledge
Lies beneath the sand and grime;
Once their cryptic hieroglyphics
Scrolled across the page of time.

As the Hittite Empire crumbled
All their secrets carved in stone
Were eventually forgotten
Left abandoned and alone.

Rulers of the mighty Mayas
Knew their answer would suffice.
They would keep their gods supplied with
Blood and human sacrifice.

But we say, "We will not perish
Cause a new thing has our vote.
We will march into the future
To a scientific note."

History waits to give the verdict
Cold, indifferent and sublime
As our cryptic hieroglyphics
Scroll across the page of time.

A Dream Undone
William F. Bell

I dreamed I saw you at the parish fair,
Laughing with others while you walked,
But you vanished around a corner
While I, unthinking, stood and talked.

Recalling your grave, ironic smile
And your way with jokes, off I sped,
Hoping to find you at the corner,
But then I remembered you were dead.

Like a flimsily built movie set,
The buildings around me came down,
And I stood in the wreck of my dream
In the midst of a shattered town,

And the spell of that desolation
Stayed with me when I awoke,
Regretting the smile I would never see
And your latest untold joke.

Two Women
William F. Bell

Something in her words I caught
As she came down the stair,
Gave surprising proof that she,
Red ribbon in her yellow hair,
Had somehow learned to care for me.
I reveled in that glorious thought.

But nothing came of it, you know,
For it would have been unfair,
No matter what I felt for her,
Red ribbon in her yellow hair,
To make of this an overture
When otherwise we differed so.

Years after, on another stair,
Another woman, a new surprise,
Descended with such charming fuss,
Happy smile and azure eyes,
Crying "lovely" and "marvelous"
And scattering joy upon the air.

I watched her with a thoughtful frown:
Could such ingenuousness be wise?
But then I learned that this odd girl,
Happy smile and azure eyes,
Could fashion sense from noise and whirl
And turn my prudence upside down.

OUR LOSS
William Ruleman

Sometimes, in the drive for brutal honesty,
we may overlook the truth, which often may shy
away from words, as cruel to the budding tree
of love as blistering noonday sun in July.
Acidic words that etch into one's soul
or eat, like a brown recluse's juice, through flesh,
critique that makes of starry-eyed hope a black hole
and the wheat of promise we've sown too shriveled to thresh.
We do our damnedest, don't we, to make ourselves heard,
and biting wit or caustic scorn suffice
to get the attention, in lieu of a gentler word.
It's true that one can't get ahead just by being "nice."
But in gaining the world we may lose what is real,
numbing our delicate power to love and feel.

The Enduring Voice:
Robert Frost in a New Century
by Richard Wakefield

In 1935, when he was sixty-one years old and had been a publishing poet for over forty years, Robert Frost wrote that he had "stayed content with the old-fashioned way to be new" even while "our age ran wild in the quest of new ways to be new." He had seen (and heard) poetry tried without form, without image, without emotion ("like murder for small pay in the underworld"), without "phrase, epigram, coherence, logic and consistency."

Well, some of the "new ways to be new" have in turn become old ways, and some of them work. E.E. Cummings, T.S. Eliot, Marianne Moore – they have their moments, more than a few. And even the flood of anarchists who poured out of post-war America, Ginsberg, say, have their moments. But there were fewer and fewer poets and moments as the decades went by, it seems to me.

One clue to the reason may be that Allen Ginsberg's favorite poem, according to many who knew him well, was not Whitman's anarchic "Song of Myself," much as he owed Whitman. It was William Wordsworth's "Intimations of Immortality from Recollections of Early Childhood." Ponder that for a moment. The raving prophet of urban angst found something deep and permanent in one of the old standards, so much so that he asked that the poem be read at his memorial service.

Those who succeeded in the various new ways to be new are rather often those who were first brought to poetry by someone being new in the old way, someone like Wordsworth in "Intimations of Immortality." The poetry they wrote retained the ghost of form. Neither they nor their audience ever really lost the need for language to preserve some little bit of order. Life itself, after all, now and then grants us a glimpse of order, of form; poets are those who use words to save it for the rest of us. Frost again: "My object is true form – form true to any chance bit of true life." And so people who have never swung skyward on a birch tree, never mended a stone wall, never stopped a horse-drawn buggy alongside snowy woods, recognize "the chance bit of true life" to which Frost's form is in turn true.

Why Frost, out of the countless poets of his generation and after? E.A. Robinson still has a following, and so does Archibald MacLeish, for that matter. But of all the poets who wrote in traditional forms none keeps a hold on contemporary readers as Frost does. You recognized the three poems alluded to above: "Birches," "Mending Wall," "Stopping by Woods on a Snowy Evening." You would have recognized perhaps half a dozen others of his. What other American poet could a writer confidently paraphrase in the assurance that almost anyone literate enough to read in the first place would know his titles, perhaps even be able to quote long excerpts?

We can begin simply by acknowledging that Robert Frost was better than almost anyone else. Even when we get past his most familiar titles we find literally dozens and dozens of poems that are masterworks. Take "The Tuft of Flowers" and the untitled poem that begins "In winter in the woods alone...," two poems written almost sixty years apart. Both precisely obey the conventions of rhyme and meter, yet both preserve the natural cadences and intonations of a real human being speaking intimately. Read one of his great blank-verse poems, "Home Burial," perhaps, or "The Death of the Hired Man," in which people converse in the everyday tones of life and yet the ironclad rules of iambic pentameter prevail for hundreds of lines. The artistry is breathtaking; the fidelity to real emotion is life giving.

There's more. When Frost began his career as a poet, in the 1890s, America and the rest of the industrializing world were caught in a great spasm of nostalgia. A poet like Eugene Field ("The Old Swimmin'-Hole," "When the Frost is on the Punkin") sold in the thousands by fulfilling the public's desire to be transported to a simpler, more innocent past, even if in fact the past had never been quite that simple or innocent. *Nostalgia* is simply Greek for "home-sickness." As people took jobs in business and industry they looked back longingly at what they thought they had lost, a life lived by the rhythms of nature (and human nature), a life scaled to the speed and sound of natural processes. Few would have gone back to it, of course. They didn't miss the labor, the isolation, the calamities of rural life. But something was wrong, they felt, with a life adjusted to the frantic pace of machinery, with voices always raised to be heard above the roar and screech of the factory and the locomotive. They were home sick.

And we are still home sick. Few of use have first hand memories of life lived at a natural pace and on a human scale, but our flesh remembers, our spirit remembers. Those little bits of form that life grants us now and then need time to take shape, and yet we hurl ourselves from moment to moment faster than the form can crystallize. It takes a poem, with its own internal pace, to slow us down and help us pay attention. One necessary condition of a successful poem might be that it cannot be fully absorbed any faster than it can be spoken.

Part of Frost's genius, I believe, is that in his poems we recognize our own yearning. They are not mere escapes into an imaginary past. They are, rather, little dramas of escape, and often of the complications of trying to escape. Consider "The Road Not Taken," with its resounding assertion of independence: "Two roads diverged in a wood, and I -- / I took the one less traveled by, / And that has made all the difference." It's a handy epigram for anyone called to speak at a high school commencement, and it pretty well expresses the way we like to feel about our own past. But look at the rest of the poem, at the speaker's uncertainty about which road really was the one less traveled, the speaker's reluctance to make any choice at all, his promise to himself that he would come back some day and explore the other road, his awareness that "way leads on to way" and that therefore, despite his promise, the alternative path would remain unknown to him. This poem stays with us because it is honest about the difficulty of going back. It is true to life. Even in memory, it tells us, we run up against our tendency to simplify a past that was in reality altogether overwhelming.

In "Mending Wall" the poet quizzes his neighbor about the need for this stone wall that the two of them repair every spring after the frost heaves of winter have scattered the rocks. And yet it is the poet himself who goes to the neighbor's house every year to tell him it is time to take up their task again. The "something" that "doesn't love a wall" is not, after all, the poet; it is nature, time, the mutability that erases human accomplishment. The poet's abortive conversation with his neighbor isn't an effort to get him to abandon their work. It is an effort to discover new purpose for an old form. He craves the form and he takes pleasure in the labor of reestablishing it, but he knows that its original reason for existing is gone. The other man falls back on a kind of nostalgia by quoting his father: "Good fences make good neighbors." They both need the wall in some way, but Frost, like us almost a hundred years later, knows that we can't completely trust ourselves when we recall the old ways of needing. We can keep the form, perhaps must keep the form, whether of a wall or of a poem, but we must discover a new use for it and a new meaning in it, ones that are true to our present lives.

Even "Birches" complicates our nostalgic impulses. For all its heart-lifting images of a boy at play, the poem tells us early on that what drew the poet back to those images is a kind of willful mistake. Those arched birches he sees and that send him into his reverie were not bent by a boy's swinging them. They were doubled over by ice storms, which "bend them down to stay," much as we are bent down by life. Yet he needs an escape "when I'm weary of considerations, / And life is too much like a pathless wood..." By the power of imagination he will form his own way through the pathless wood, back to a simpler time, but he never forgets that the real world has other plans for him, and he never lets us forget it either, at least not for long.

Despite its being about a situation that was already anachronistic by the time Frost wrote it, "Stopping by Woods on a Snowy Evening" seems to me one of the best poems ever written about what it feels like to be alive today, almost a hundred years later. Who has not yearned to turn aside and contemplate nature, only to be drawn away by the internalized voices of "promises to keep"? Granted, the poem is about a seemingly simpler time, when people got around by buggy and when tracts of undisturbed forest still dotted the landscape, but the speaker in the poem is much like us. His homesickness is very real, but he lives in a world that offers no simple cure.

Except, perhaps, the poem itself. There, for sixteen precious lines, we can hear the "sweep / Of easy wind," feel the "downy flake." The sound of our insistent promises is not absent, but it is muted enough to allow us to hear the craving of our spirit for the sounds and sights of nature. That is how we experience nature today as we teeter on the brink of a new millennium, in moments stolen from the insistent hustle of modern life. A poem, especially a poem that uses the old familiar forms, can be one of those stolen moments.

In the late 1950s the critic Lionel Trilling needed to justify his admiration of Frost's poetry. As a scholar he apparently felt that it would be declasse to like the poetry for the same reasons that great numbers of unsophisticated readers did, and so he declared that he had discovered Frost to be "a terrifying poet." Among the poems he cited was "Desert Places," which is indeed not without evidence of a spiritual crisis. Yet I believe general readers had long before recognized and responded to this element of Frost's poetry. No one had felt the need to reduce it to such an unambiguous term as "terrifying," though, because sensitive readers have always sensed that it is intricately interwoven with every other element in his work, as it is in our lives.

We are at heart ambivalent creatures, and when we long for the serenity of the winter woods we also fear the consequences of indulging our longing. Who will do the work, pay the bills, fulfill the obligations? The poems allow us a rather free play of emotions, so with any given reading the sense of fear or reluctance may register more or less strongly. This is why Robert Frost's poetry grows with us, becomes an organic part of us, and even becomes, as another critic has put it, a tool for living. The brief interval of a Frost poem can be a refuge, but never a false one.

Frost said once that a successful poet is one who "has fitted into the nature of mankind." The brief but large success of other poets, from Eugene Field to Rod McCuen, suggests that they fitted into at least some part of the nature of mankind. The enduring voice of Robert Frost, however, fits our nature whole, with all its desires and complications, all its mystery. In ways we can only dimly sense we are bound to nature, to one another, and perhaps to something even greater. Frost's poems give form to our intimations, not so much to explain them as to allow us to experience them afresh:

> And God has taken a flower of gold
> > And broken it, and used therefrom
> The mystic link to bind and hold
> > Spirit to matter till death come.

Index of Contributors
[Listed in order of first appearance]